IMAGES
of America

UNIVERSITY AVENUE
OF THE TWIN CITIES

IMAGES
of America

UNIVERSITY AVENUE
OF THE TWIN CITIES

Iric Nathanson

ARCADIA
PUBLISHING

Published by Arcadia Publishing
Charleston, South Carolina

Printed in the United States of America

Library of Congress Control Number: 2022947158

For all general information, please contact Arcadia Publishing:
Telephone 843-853-2070
Fax 843-853-0044
E-mail sales@arcadiapublishing.com
For customer service and orders:
Toll-Free 1-888-313-2665

Visit us on the Internet at www.arcadiapublishing.com

To Marlene

CONTENTS

ACKNOWLEDGMENTS

Over the past year, as this book took shape, many people helped make *University Avenue of the Twin Cities* a reality. Longtime St. Paul historian Jane McClure reviewed my early draft and offered useful suggestions that did much to improve my narrative. Ted Hathaway and his staff at the Hennepin County Library Special Collections located many of the archival images reproduced on the following pages. I was also able to access historic photographs with the help of Rich Arpi with the Ramsey County Historical Society, Aaron Isaacs with Minnesota Streetcar Museum, and Rebecca Toov with the University of Minnesota archives. Caitrin Cunningham, my editor at Arcadia Publishing, kept me on track as this project moved from the idea stage to the final product. And finally, my wife, Marlene, provided support and encouragement during those long hours that I spent hunched over my computer. All images are courtesy of the Minnesota Historical Society unless otherwise noted.

INTRODUCTION

University Avenue begins its journey through the Twin Cities in northeast Minneapolis, once a port of entry for Eastern European immigrants. The street moves on through the campus of the University of Minnesota and the adjoining Prospect Park neighborhood. As it reaches the top of Tower Hill, marked by the distinctive water tower known as the Witch's Hat, University Avenue continues into St. Paul, through the Midway District, and on past the Minnesota State Capitol before ending abruptly on St. Paul's east side.

Historically, the avenue's 13 miles have served as a connector linking Minnesota's two adjoining urban centers. The state's earliest maps, dating to the 1840s, show a trail connecting the two frontier settlements that would become the state's major cities. But it would take roughly another 30 years for construction to begin on a roadway along the route now known as University Avenue.

Public transportation appeared on the new thoroughfare in the 1880s in the form of horse-drawn trolley cars. In 1890, the street railway companies in both cities came together to build an electrified streetcar line along University Avenue that connected the two downtowns. Known as the Interurban, it became the most popular trolley line in the Twin Cities, with cars running along its route every three minutes. The Interurban line helped boost University Avenue as a major commercial and industrial corridor. Starting in the early years of the last century, factories, shops, and restaurants sprang up in clusters around the street's major intersections.

At Lexington Avenue, a baseball park bearing that street's name anchored the intersection for nearly 60 years. Lexington Park was the home of the St. Paul Saints, longtime rivals of the Minneapolis Millers ball club, which had a home field seven miles away at Nicollet Park. After Lexington Park closed, the Saints moved to a new home near the Minnesota State Fair grounds.

Down the street from the University Avenue ballpark, the Prom Ballroom was the place to see and be seen on Saturday night. For nearly 50 years, the Prom served as a venue for a wide range of musical acts in genres ranging from to rock to polka to jazz. The ballroom's many fans mourned its closing when the building was demolished in 1987.

During the early decades of the 20th century, University Avenue emerged as St. Paul's automobile row as dealers representing all the major companies chose to locate there. At its high point in the 1950s, University Avenue was home to more than 20 new car dealerships.

Through the 1950s, the avenue continued to serve as the major destination for Twin Citians who came to the intercity thoroughfare to work, shop, and play. But the street's fortunes began to decline in the 1960s, when a new intercity freeway, Interstate 94, connected the two downtowns. This 11-mile freeway connection was linked to a broader metro area highway network and enabled industries, retailers, and residents to flee the central cities and move to the suburbs, where land was cheaper and development was less congested. Interstate 94 delivered a death blow to University Avenue's "auto row." One by one, the dealers abandoned the avenue and built new, up-to-date showrooms in St. Paul's first and second ring suburbs.

During those same years of the 1960s, major commercial businesses along University Avenue, including the massive Montgomery Ward complex, began to close. However, a new era in the street's development was about to begin as new arrivals to Minnesota—many from Southeast Asia—injected fresh entrepreneurial energy into the aging urban corridor.

By the 1980s, Minnesota was attracting refugees fleeing a Communist-dominated Vietnam. Through the resettlement work of the Lutheran Social Services and other local social service agencies, Minnesota became a center of Vietnamese American life. Many of these new Minnesotans opened restaurants and other businesses on University Avenue. Another wave of Southeast Asian refugees came to St. Paul in the 1980s and 1990s, when many Hmong people from Laos resettled in Minnesota. Like the Vietnamese, many Hmong families opened retail and service businesses along University Avenue.

The second decade of the 21st century brought another major change for University Avenue when construction began on the Central Corridor light rail transit (LRT) line. Now known as the Green Line, the LRT sparked a construction boom around the 12 stations located on the corridor. With support from public agencies and nonprofit community groups, the corridor's neighborhood-based businesses were able to contend with the three years of disruption caused by the construction of the Green Line.

Now, in the third decade of the 21st century, the face of University Avenue continues to change as multistory residential and commercial developments replace the original century-old buildings along the street. New private and public investment is helping to restore University Avenue's traditional role as a major connector linking Minneapolis and St. Paul.

One

FLAGSHIP INSTITUTION

University Avenue had not yet appeared on street maps of the Twin Cities when the first building, known as Old Main, was constructed on what would later become the University of Minnesota's main campus. Old Main, a three-story gray stone structure, was completed in 1858 but remained vacant for nine years because the university had run out of funds during the Civil War and was forced to close. When the school's fortunes were revived, Old Main finally opened in 1867. By 1880, when University Avenue was paved, the school's enrollment had reached 300; twenty years later, in 1900, that number had exceeded 1,000. Over the next 120 years, the university continued to grow, with the Minneapolis campus covering more than 1,200 acres and student enrollment topping 36,000.

Several of the Minneapolis campus's most historic buildings continue to line University Avenue. These include Sanford Hall (named for the university's first female professor, Maria Sanford) and Folwell Hall (named for the school's first president, William Watts Folwell).

Starting in the 1920s, the north side of University Avenue adjacent to the campus became the home of fraternities and sororities at the center of the university's social life. Many of these buildings continue to be identified by their Greek letters. University Avenue's most iconic campus structure, Memorial Stadium—the home of the Golden Gopher football team—is now a thing of the past, as the 60,000-seat stadium was demolished in 1992. Huntington Bank Stadium, located down the block on University Avenue, now serves as the home of the Golden Gophers.

This ornamental gate on University Avenue serves as the entrance to oldest section of the University of Minnesota, originally known as the Knoll. Now identified as the University of Minnesota Old Campus Historic District, the area includes a collection of buildings dating from the 1880s and 1890s. With its broad lawn and curving streets, the Knoll presents an image of a bucolic college campus from the time when the 19th century turned into the 20th. (Courtesy of the University of Minnesota Archives.)

Minnesota philanthropist and business leader John S. Pillsbury was a key University of Minnesota benefactor during the school's early years. The founder of the milling company that bears his name, Pillsbury served as president of the university's board of regents following his three terms as governor of Minnesota. Pillsbury is often called the "father of the university." (Courtesy of the University of Minnesota Archives.)

Pillsbury Hall, dating to 1889, is a prime example of Richardsonian Romanesque architecture. The building is noted for its use of contrasting red and beige sandstone. Pillsbury Hall is one of two structures on the University of Minnesota campus named for John S. Pillsbury. (Courtesy of the University of Minnesota Archives.)

The acclaimed American sculptor Daniel Chester French created this imposing bronze statue of John S. Pillsbury. The statute was erected in 1900 in appreciation of Pillsbury's service to the University of Minnesota. The monument is located on the Knoll in the University of Minnesota Old Campus Historic District. (Courtesy of the University of Minnesota Archives.)

William Watts Folwell was born in New York and served on the faculty of Ohio's Kenyon College before moving to Minnesota to take the helm of the state's land grant institution of higher education. When Folwell became the first president of the University of Minnesota in 1867, the school had only 8 faculty members and 100 students. (Courtesy of the University of Minnesota Archives.)

The block-length building shown here under construction is named for William Folwell, the first president of the University of Minnesota. The highly ornamental Folwell Hall served as the university's primary classroom building following the fire that destroyed Old Main in 1904. Architectural historian Larry Millett described Folwell Hall as "a Tudor Jacobean romance, gorgeous ornamented in terra cotta." (Courtesy of the University of Minnesota Archives.)

In the 1950s and 1960s, Folwell Hall was the home of the University of Minnesota English Department. During those years, several prominent literary figures were members of the department's faculty, including Robert Penn Warren, John Berryman, and Saul Bellow. This well-dressed young couple may have attended a lecture by one of these distinguished faculty members. (Courtesy of the University of Minnesota Archives.)

Dating to 1910, Sanford Hall was the University of Minnesota's first dormitory designed to accommodate women. In 1964, a tower was added to the original building to increase its capacity to 502 residents. Sanford Hall is now a co-ed dormitory. (Courtesy of the University of Minnesota Archives.)

This residence hall is named for Maria Sanford, a nationally prominent educator and one of the first women to obtain a college-level faculty position. During her 30-year career at the University of Minnesota, Sanford taught rhetoric, literature, and art history. She was also a conservation activist who helped spearhead the creation of the Superior National Forest in northern Minnesota. (Courtesy of the University of Minnesota Archives.)

The University of Minnesota honored one of its most illustrious graduates, Roy Wilkins, by naming this residence hall after him. Wilkins spent his formative years in St. Paul's Rondo Neighborhood, later graduating from the university with a degree in sociology. As executive director of the National Association for the Advancement of Colored People (NAACP), Wilkins became one of the country's most prominent civil rights leaders during the tumultuous 1960s and 1970s. (Above, courtesy of the author; left, courtesy of the University of Minnesota Archives.)

The 66,000-seat Memorial Stadium served as the home of the University of Minnesota's football team, the Golden Gophers, from 1924 to 1981. During their years at Memorial Stadium, the Gophers won three consecutive national championships starting in 1934. This aerial scene shows a game in progress in 1955. Memorial Stadium was demolished in 1992. An aquatic building and an alumni center now occupy the former site of the stadium. (Both, courtesy of the University of Minnesota Archives.)

A native Minnesotan, Bernie Bierman was the head football coach at the University of Minnesota from 1932 to 1950. During his legendary coaching career, the Golden Gophers won five national championships and seven Big Ten conference titles. Bierman is pictured with the team in 1932, his first year as Minnesota's head coach. (Courtesy of the University of Minnesota Archives.)

During homecoming week each fall, the University of Minnesota fraternities try to outdo each other with elaborate decorations in their houses' front yards. Delta Tau Delta's Paul Bunyan is shown "Blasting the Purdue Boilermakers" in 1949. That year, the Gophers lost to Purdue 7-13. (Courtesy of the University of Minnesota Archives.)

The history of the University of Minnesota's gopher mascot goes back to 1857, when Minnesota was labeled the "Gopher State" by a cartoonist who was satirizing the Minnesota legislature. In the 1930s, the adjective "golden" was added to the mascot's name after a sportscaster noted that the university's football players were wearing golden pants and jerseys. (Courtesy of the University of Minnesota Archives.)

19

This PWA Moderne building was constructed in 1940 to house the University of Minnesota's Bell Museum of Natural History. The sculpture above the entrance depicts a buffalo roaming the prairie. In 2009, the museum was moved to a new building on the St. Paul campus. The former museum now houses offices for the university's Institute of Technology. (Courtesy of the University of Minnesota Archives.)

Named for legendary football coach Dr. Henry Williams, Williams Arena was known as "the barn" when it was built in 1928. At the time, it was one of the county's largest college sports arenas and could seat 18,000 fans. In 1993, the building was modernized and updated.

The castle-like Armory was built in 1896 to house the University of Minnesota's military science program. Referring to the Armory's parapet, architectural historian Larry Millett said, "you half expect to see archers or maybe the guys with boiling oil preparing for an attack." The statue in this photograph is known as *Iron Jack* and was built in 1906 to commemorate university students who served in the Spanish-American War. (Courtesy of the University of Minnesota Archives.)

The University of Minnesota YMCA traces its origins to 1887, when 13 charter members organized the campus branch. The early branch was housed on campus in the Men's Union Building. In the mid-1920s, the University Y moved into this Gothic-style building at 1425 University Avenue. (Courtesy of Hennepin County Library Special Collections.)

Known to generations of University of Minnesota students as the Dinkdome, this classically embellished building was constructed in 1915 for the Minnesota Bible College. The building gets its name from its distinctive domed roof. In 2009, the Dinkdome was redeveloped as an apartment building with a 10-story addition. (Both, courtesy of Hennepin County Library Special Collections.)

Two

MINNESOTA
STATE CAPITOL

Construction of University Avenue was still decades in the future when Minnesota's first state capitol was built in 1854 in what is now downtown St. Paul. When this modest structure was destroyed by fire, a second state capitol was built on the same site. But it was soon outmoded, prompting calls for a more expansive capitol building that could meet the needs of a fast-growing state.

When planning began for the current Minnesota capitol building in 1883, University Avenue had recently been paved; it would later serve as the route of the Interurban car line. The new state capitol building opened in 1905, with University Avenue skirting its perimeter.

Visitors travelling down University Avenue to reach the capitol had another reason to visit the imposing building, even if they were not particularly interested in the proceedings on the House and Senate floors. They could come to the capitol to drink beer in an authentic rathskeller decorated with German drinking slogans—a friendly amenity in many Germanic government buildings. However, the capitol rathskeller was short-lived. With the advent of World War I, when German culture was considered anti-American, the cafe was closed, and its slogans were covered with layers of white paint. In the 1990s, the rathskeller was reopened and restored to its original 1905 appearance.

Many of the dignitaries who attended the 1896 ground-breaking ceremony for the new Minnesota State Capitol may have travelled down University Avenue to reach the construction site. The man in shirtsleeves holding the shovel is Channing Seabury, vice president of the Board of State Capitol Commissioners. Seabury was responsible for steering the capitol construction plan through a politically contentious approval process.

St. Paul architect Cass Gilbert had made a name for himself building homes for the city's affluent residents when his firm was hired to design Minnesota's new state capitol. Gilbert's design was well received and boosted him into the ranks of the country's leading early-20th-century architects. His other notable designs include the US Supreme Court and New York City's Woolworth Building.

In a design competition managed by the Board of State Capitol Commissioners, Cass Gilbert competed with other prominent local architects for the contract to design the new seat of Minnesota state government. After deliberating for two days, the commissioners selected Gilbert's firm. A drawing of Gilbert's plan is shown in this staff photograph. Gilbert is in the center of the group; he is seated and wearing a bow tie.

May 9 1901

Cass Gilbert is shown here in 1901 inspecting the construction of the partially completed capitol. Early in the building's planning process, Gilbert was embroiled in a controversy when he decreed that Georgia marble would be used for the capitol exterior, ignoring critics who wanted Minnesota building materials to be used. Gilbert prevailed, but he did agree to use Minnesota sandstone for capitol dome's piers and foundations.

The capitol's most prominent feature, its massive dome, is entirely self-supporting. The dome is second in size only to the dome on St. Peter's Basilica in Rome. Historian Denis Gardner says that the "richly ornamented dome is reminiscent of a bejeweled papal tiara. . . . Its final garnish is a lantern with a shining global finial."

The cornerstone-laying ceremony for the capitol was held on July 27, 1898, and was a major community event. Former territorial governor Alexander Ramsey, then 83 years old, was the guest of honor. A time capsule embedded in the stone contained historic photographs and documents.

A BIG TIME IS ARRANGED

OLD ST. PAUL WILL JUBILATE

The Complete Program for Capitol Cornerstone Festivities Is Made Public.

As the 1898 capitol cornerstone-laying ceremony was in the preparation phase, the *Minneapolis Journal* reported that "the committees in charge of the work of arranging for the ceremonies and festivities in connection with the laying of the cornerstone has done their job well. Nothing remains now but to await the hour set for the occasion which will be long remembered by the residents of Minnesota who will be there."

THE CONTEMPLATIVE SPIRIT OF THE EAST
BY KENYON COX.

A staunch advocate for public art, architect Cass Gilbert told the Minnesota State Capitol commissioners that "nothing will give this building greater distinction . . . than the recognition of the arts as represented by the greater painters and sculptors of the present day." Gilbert was able to persuade the commissioners to allocate $300,000—7 percent of the capitol's total construction budget—for public art, including this mural in the Senate chamber.

In designing the informal dining area on the capitol's ground floor known as the rathskeller, architect Cass Gilbert copied the Germanic practice of locating restaurants in the basements (*keller* in German) of city halls (*rathaus* in German). The capitol's rathskeller was not around for long. With the advent of World War I came an upsurge of anti-German sentiment, and the restaurant was closed. In the 1990s, the rathskeller was restored to its original appearance.

Civil War veterans are shown in 1905 carrying battle flags from the old Minnesota capitol building on Tenth Avenue to the new state capitol. Civil War commemorations were an important part of the capitol's decor. Two paintings in the governor's reception room depict Civil War battles in which Minnesota soldiers, fighting for the Union, played a key role. (Courtesy of Hennepin County Library Special Collections.)

When the newly completed capitol was opened to the public for the first time in January 1905, the *Minneapolis Tribune* declared: "Minnesota can well be proud of her new capitol building. It is a structure built for all time. The building is constructed on classical lines and is surmounted by a dome that has few equals in design in the country."

Three

LOST LANDMARKS

Over the last 50 years, University Avenue has undergone a major transformation. The changes have led to the loss of important landmarks that helped define this key intercity transportation corridor. A notable loss occurred with the demolition of the 257-foot-high tower that marked the location of Montgomery Ward's retail store and distribution center. The massive complex, built in 1921, included an administrative wing that was later converted to a retail store and an eight-story warehouse. When the 1921 complex was demolished in 1995, it was replaced by a new 100,000-square-foot Wards retail store. The new Wards building included a 70-foot-high replica of the original tower.

Down the road from Wards, Lexington Park brought baseball fans flocking to University Avenue for nearly 60 years. Dating to 1897, the stadium was the home of the St. Paul Saints baseball team. After Lexington Park closed in 1956, the Saints moved to a new home near the Minnesota State Fair grounds.

Porky's Drive-In, one of University Avenue's best-known landmarks, survived until 2011. For more than 50 years, Porky's was the place to go for hamburgers, french fries, and malts. The drive-in, with its distinctive checkerboard facade, was built in 1953 at a time when roadside businesses vied with each other to attract attention.

While University Avenue has lost landmarks, the street is creating a new identity for itself in the 21st century.

Minneapolis's Eastgate Shopping Center opened in 1955 at the intersection of University and Central Avenues. The $750,000 strip development was anchored by a Red Owl grocery store with off-street parking for 125 cars. Eastgate was demolished in 2004. A condominium building with a Lunds & Byerlys grocery store on the first floor now occupies the site. (Above, courtesy of Hennepin County Library Special Collections.)

A Coca-Cola bottling plant occupied the former site of the Minneapolis Exposition Building. The plant was in operation from 1946 until the mid-1980s, when it was demolished as part of a city redevelopment project. The property remained vacant until 1994, when the Lourdes Square townhouse development was built on the site. (Courtesy of Hennepin County Library Special Collections.)

For more than 50 years, this classic drive-in was one of University Avenue's most widely recognized landmarks. Porky's University Avenue eatery was one of the last remaining drive-in restaurants in the Twin Cities. When Porky's closed in 2011, the building was moved to the Log House Antique Farm near Hastings, Minnesota.

According to architectural historian Larry Millett, "With his top hat tilted at a rakish angle, Porky's [was] one of University Avenue's most beloved icons." Porky's was "authentically garish, down to the last detail." The drive-in's checkerboard facade was its most distinctive feature.

The New Northwest Home
of
Montgomery Ward & Company

When Montgomery Ward's new facility on University Avenue opened in April 1921, the 1.2-million-square-foot complex was St. Paul's largest commercial development up to that time. The complex included an administrative wing that was later converted to a retail store and an eight-story warehouse and distribution center. The complex was imploded in 1996 and replaced with a new 100,000-square-foot Wards store. That site is now part of a development known as the Midway Marketplace.

Interesting Facts About Our Twin Cty House

Our 257-foot tower—the highest concrete tower in the world. Our 115,000-gallon sprinkling tank. Our floor space equals in size a 17-acre farm. 90 miles of electric wiring in our building. 4,100 men worked on the construction of our Twin City plant.

This 1921 Montgomery Ward advertisement in the *Pioneer Press* provided details about the company's new Midwest facility. Wards boasted that the building's signature tower, at 257 feet, was the largest concrete sculpture of its type in the world. Wards also reported that the St. Paul center had floor space equal to that of a 17-acre farm. (Courtesy of the University of Minnesota Libraries.)

Montgomery Ward's St. Paul distribution center, known as a catalogue house, was one of the company's first such facilities built outside of Chicago. This image shows merchandise being loaded onto a delivery truck at the back of the building. The slogan on the truck reads: "Satisfaction guaranteed or your money back."

These young men had one of the most highly prized jobs at Montgomery Ward—they got paid to spend their work shifts on roller skates. The skates had a practical use. With the building's 17 acres of floor space, skates helped the workers move around more quickly than they could in shoes.

BALLROOM
RAY   WINKLER TONITE
RANDY   BROOKS   WED
GEORGE   WINSLOW   THUR

Starting in 1941, when it opened, the Prom Ballroom was the place to see and be seen on a Saturday night. Over its 40-year history, the Prom hosted many legendary orchestras. In 1965, bandleaders Jules Herman and Louis Armstrong appeared there. The Prom's many fans mourned its closing when the building was demolished in 1987.

These young people are participating in the St. Paul Winter Carnival dance contest at the Prom Ballroom in 1965. The young lady is looking ahead intently as her partner whirls her around the floor. Throughout the 1960s, dance contests were a highlight of St. Paul's midwinter celebrations.

The Criterion brought fine dining to University Avenue from the 1940s through the 1970s. The restaurant featured a lobster tank where patrons could select their own seafood entree. This advertisement includes a drawing of the restaurant's signature dish. In 1978, the Criterion's University Avenue building was destroyed in a fire. (Above, courtesy of Ramsey County Historical Society.)

Nationally Admired
the Criterion Restaurant
739 University Avenue at Grotto
Saint Paul, Minnesota

Lexington Park was the home of the St. Paul Saints baseball club from 1897 through 1956. The park was located on the southwest corner of Lexington Parkway and University Avenue. Charles Comiskey, the legendary owner of the Chicago White Sox, built Lexington Park at a time when he also owned the St. Paul club. Comiskey's involvement in Twin Cities baseball was short-lived, however. In 1909, he sold the Saints and their ballpark to a local financial group.

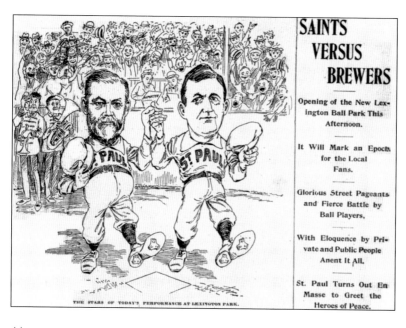

In this *Pioneer Press* drawing, two unnamed St. Paul Saints baseball players clasp hands as they prepare to do battle with the Milwaukee Brewers on opening day at Lexington Park in 1897. The 8,000 fans who filled the new ballpark for that first game were able to see their hometown team defeat the Brewers 10-3.

Officials are shown consulting with representatives from the St. Paul Saints and the Minneapolis Millers prior to the first intercity game at Lexington Park in 1926. Through the early 1950s, the two teams often played each other twice in one day in what were known as streetcar doubleheaders. A morning game would be played at one team's home field. Later in the day, the second game was played at the other team's home field.

The 1937 St. Paul Saints season made history when Lexington Park got lights. That year, the first night game was played on July 15, with the Saints hosting their archrivals, the Minneapolis Millers. The teams played again the next night in Nicollet Park's first night game.

Lexington Park
To See Last Ball Game

Lexington ball park will end its 59-year baseball domination in St. Paul Wednesday night when the Saints close the home season against Minneapolis. Then the stadium will be torn down and the Saints will begin the 1957 season in the new stadium on Snelling.

At their final game at Lexington Park on September 5, 1956, the St. Paul Saints defeated the Minneapolis Millers 4-0. Despite the win by the hometown team, Lexington Park did not go out in a blaze of glory, according to baseball historian Stew Thornley. Fewer than 3,000 fans turned out for the final game, which was held on a cold and rainy September night.

Four

ECONOMIC ENGINE

Two buildings at either end of St. Paul's University Avenue symbolize the street's industrial past. At the west end, a massive block-length structure dominates the intersection with Highway 280. To the east, a more modest three-story building sits in the shadow of the Minnesota State Capitol.

The two structures, which are located six miles apart, were once automobile assembly plants. The larger of the two, the office building now known as Court International, was built in 1915 for the Willys-Overland Company. The smaller building, which dates to 1914, is now vacant and threatened with demolition, although it originally served as a distribution center for the Ford Motor Company. Ford later moved its Minnesota operation to a massive new plant in St. Paul's Highland Park neighborhood. Ford soon outgrew the 1914 building, but many local industrial firms were able to remain at their original University Avenue locations through the first half of the 20th century.

As University Avenue's industrial era began to come to an end in the 1970s, many of the early structures started to be repurposed as office buildings, apartments, and condominiums. The avenue's new role as a light rail corridor in the early 2000s spurred the adaptive reuse of these older buildings and helped to preserve a significant part of the avenue's early-20th-century history.

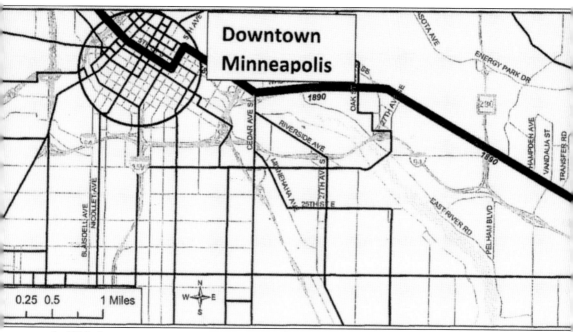

In 1890, the streetcar companies in Minneapolis and St. Paul—which were soon to be merged into the Twin City Rapid Transit Company (TCRT)—completed a trolley line connecting the two downtown areas. Known as the Interurban, the line ran along University Avenue for most of its

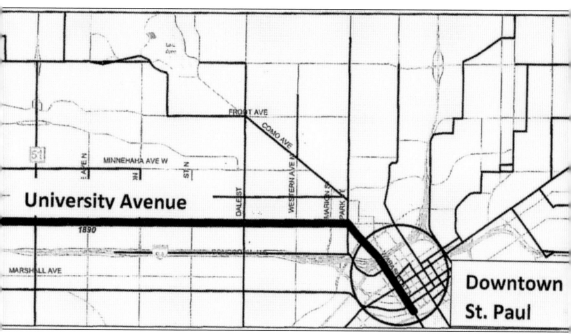

10-mile route. The Interurban soon become one of TCRT's most popular lines, with cars running every three minutes during rush hour. Local historian Aaron Isaacs attributes the Midway District's success as a commercial and industrial hub to the Interurban line. (Courtesy of Aaron Isaacs.)

New Address...

for A FAMILIAR NAME IN THE TWIN CITIES

ACCOUNTING MACHINES

ELECTRIC TYPEWRITERS

PUNCHED-CARD METHODS

PRINTING CALCULATORS

RECORD PHOTOGRAPHY

VISIBLE SYSTEMS

ADDING MACHINES

SAFE-FILES, SAFE-CABINETS

SUPER-RITER TYPEWRITERS

VERTICAL FILING EQUIPMENT

RIBBONS, CARBONS

OFFICE FURNITURE

CATALOG BINDERS

NOISELESS TYPEWRITERS

INDUSTRIAL TELEVISION

DUPLICATOR SUPPLIES

PORTABLE TYPEWRITERS

ELECTRIC SHAVERS

REMINGTON RAND

OPENS COMPLETE NEW
BUSINESS EQUIPMENT CENTER
AT 3300 UNIVERSITY AVENUE, S. E. MINNEAPOLIS 14

Minneapolis Telephone No.: Fillmore 5501 • St. Paul Telephone No.: Prior 3419

To give Minneapolis and St. Paul businessmen and government officials the finest possible facilities for viewing and buying our world-famous lines of products for better living," Remington Rand announces the opening of a new Business Equipment Center in our own building at 3300 University Ave., S.E., Minneapolis—centrally located mid-way between the Twin Cities for your convenience.

For ways of making machines, systems and equipment work together for greatest efficiency and dollar return...your best bet is Remington Rand...because ...we aren't limited to any one system or machine when it comes to solving your business problems!

Why not make our new Sales Center your headquarters for business service? It's the place where you can discuss your cost-cutting problems on a "prove-it-to-me" basis. No obligation, of course.

Remington Rand

THE FIRST NAME IN BUSINESS SYSTEMS

3300 University Avenue, S. E., Minneapolis 14, Minn.

For your needs we have no reason to recommend anything but the right machines and systems. We make them all

Established in 1927 through the merger of Remington Typewriter Company and the Rand Karday Company, Remington Rand emerged as a major producer of office equipment in the 1930s and 1940s. This sales center opened on University Avenue in 1952. The center sold a broad range of office products, including typewriters, calculators, and duplicators. (Courtesy of Hennepin County Library Special Collections.)

In this June 1952 advertisement, Remington Rand declared that its new equipment center was intended to give Minneapolis and St. Paul businesses and government officials "the finest possible facility for viewing and buying our world-famous lines of products for better living." It went on to note that the company's building at 3300 University Avenue was located conveniently between the Twin Cities. (Courtesy of Hennepin County Library.)

Local television station KSTP occupies the only building in the Twin Cities that straddles the Minneapolis–St. Paul boundary. The building has two zip codes and two water and electrical lines. Owned and operated by the Hubbard family, KSTP was the first station in Minnesota to provide television broadcasting service. (Courtesy of Hennepin County Library Special Collections.)

The KSTP production studios are on the Minneapolis side of the building, while the business and advertising offices are on the St. Paul side. KSTP's 594-foot transmission tower has one leg in each city and a third leg on the city line. (Courtesy of Hennepin County Library Special Collections.)

This University Avenue building was used an auto assembly plant when it was developed by the Toledo-based Willys-Overland Company in 1915. At the time, Willys-Overland was the second-largest automobile manufacturer in the United States (after Ford). In the mid-1920s, International Harvester purchased the plant and converted it into a parts and distribution center.

In the 1980s, the International Harvester plant was repurposed as an office building and renamed Court International. Today, the building looks much as it did when it was erected in 1915. (Courtesy of the author.)

A Shipment of Brand-New Overlands

950

ompletely
quipped

k. Toledo, O.

$1075

With electric
starter and
generator

f. o. b. Toledo, O.

Just arrived. Yours is here. Act today.

WE want to publicly apologize to the thousands of patient people who have been unable to get their Overland on the specified delivery date.

The situation has simply been beyond our control. Never before, during the entire history of our ever-expanding business, have orders exceeded our production program to such an astonishing extent as they have this season.

Shipping orders have poured into the factory on the average of from 500 to 600 cars a day—often running as high as 1000 cars a day.

However, this congestion is now relieved for we have been able to increase our factory production—and Overlands are now being shipped at the rate of 50 to 60 carloads a day.

Therefore, if you act promptly—by getting in touch with our dealer without further loss of time—you can be assured of an immediate delivery. Your Overland is ready to deliver to you right now.

We earnestly advise you not to wait until the demand again gets ahead of our increased production. Quick action means that tomorrow you can be enjoying your new Overland. And, what is more, you will know that you have secured the most economical and efficient popular priced car ever manufactured.

Make your arrangements today for a demonstration.

Remember, this is America's greatest motor car value. The Overland is a big, powerful, snappy, beautiful, comfortable, large, roomy car. And it is priced at 30% less than any other similar car made.

Bowman & Libby, Inc., 1203-1205 Hennepin Ave., Minneapolis.
The second largest Overland Distributers in the World.

The Willys-Overland Company, Toledo, Ohio

Manufacturers of the famous Overland Delivery Wagons, Gerford and Willys Utility Trucks.   Full information on request.

This Willys-Overland Company advertisement states: "Remember, this is America's greatest motor car value. The Overland is a big, powerful, snappy, beautiful, comfortable, large, roomy car. And it is priced at 30% less than any other similar car made."

Bisected by University Avenue, the Midway District was not yet fully developed in this 1928 aerial photograph. The four-story building at the center of the photograph housed the Griggs Cooper Company, one of the Twin Cities' largest manufacturers of food products. In the following decades, the Midway District would emerge as a key industrial center.

Railroad magnate James J. Hill was the prime mover behind the development of the Minnesota Transfer Railway. The massive facility sprawled over a 200-acre site filled with equipment that could transfer goods between a dozen railway companies serving the Twin Cities. By 1912, the Minnesota Transfer Railway consisted of 82 miles of track, 400 switches, and 19 locomotives.

The Interurban State Bank occupied the corner office in the Northwestern Furniture Exposition Building. The bank's name referred to the Interurban streetcar line; its tracks are visible in the foreground of this 1920 photograph.

The exterior of the Northwestern Furniture Exposition Building has changed little over 100 years. Today, the building overlooks the contemporary version of the Interurban line—the Green Line LRT. (Courtesy of the author.)

The Patterson Sargent Paint Company traces its origins to 1890. Calling its product lines BPS (Best Paint Sold), Patterson Sargent manufactured paints, lacquers, varnishes, and stains. In 1959, the business was purchased by the Pittsburgh-based H.K. Porter Company. Located at 2295 University Avenue, the Patterson Sargent building has now been converted to loft apartments. (Below, courtesy of the author.)

Do You Know Why Your Face Powder Doesn't "Stick"?

It is not necessary to be constantly dabbing powder on your face. So many women do this, that it has become a habit with many—an unnecessary habit—since good face powder. the proper face powder—with the proper base to hold it on—should stick all day long!

Cinderella Foundation Cream

This remarkable preparation makes your face powder stick. It provides the proper base for it. It is part of the secret of Cinderella Face Powder and its ability to stick on all day. If you are having any difficulty making your powder stick, try Cinderella Foundation Lotion. Put it on first—as directed—then apply your powder. You'll find the results very gratifying. And if you should not be satisfied, then you must look to the powder you use. Try a box of Cinderella Face Powder with our Foundation Cream—for which it was expressively made—and you will be sure to be satisfied.

"Fill In" With Cinderella

There is a correct and distinct Cinderella Cosmetic for every known type—both for day and for evening wear. Start with a few of the Cinderella Cosmetics—if you don't care to buy a complete day or evening set—and note the difference Cinderella will make in your appearance. You'll understand why it is the favorite cosmetic of many of the famous stars of the screen and stage.

CINDERELLA COSMETICS ARE FOR SALE AT ALL LEADING DRUG AND DEPARTMENT STORES

For "Her" Christmas Gift

Here's a Christmas gift that every woman will appreciate—a complete set of Cinderella Cosmetics—for her own particular type—for either day or evening wear—or—if you want to make it a super gift—BOTH! Prescription requests obtainable at all good drug and department stores. Correct prescription will be sent you by Mr. V. E. Meadows, famous cosmetician.

XX6

CINDERELLA COSMETICS
Created By
Sinykin

In this holiday advertisement, the University Avenue–based Cinderella Cosmetics Company declared, "There is a correct and distinct Cinderella Cosmetic for every known type, for day and evening wear. Start with a few of the Cinderella Cosmetics and note what a difference Cinderella will make in your appearance. You'll understand why it is the favorite cosmetic of many famous stars of stage and screen." (Courtesy of Hennepin County Library.)

This fanciful fan Art Deco building was a perfect fit for the Cinderella Cosmetics Company, which used glamour to sell its beauty products. Cinderella Cosmetics staged a grand opening for its University Avenue building on October 6, 1930, declaring that "it will be marked with the splendor and dignity of a Hollywood motion picture premier." By the 1970s, the Cinderella Cosmetics Building had been replaced by a one-story warehouse-style structure.

The Griggs Cooper Company was one of the Twin Cities' largest manufacturers of food products. At its apex, the company occupied 500,000 square feet of space at the corner of University and Fairview Avenues. In 1956, the St. Paul firm was purchased by the Chicago-based Wirtz Beverage Company. A wing of the Griggs Cooper Company is shown here under construction in 1923.

In the 1980s, the Griggs Cooper plant was converted to an office building. The current facility has retained the facade and footprint of the original factory, which was built over a 14-year period from 1911 to 1925. (Courtesy of the author.)

The Griggs Cooper Company considered itself part of the "Model Factory Movement" of the 1920s and 1930s. The nationwide movement stressed the importance of providing a positive working environment for company employees, such as the man and woman shown working in the firm's food-preparation division.

St. Paul's most prominent commercial district outside of downtown was located at Snelling and University Avenues. By the 1950s, more than 50 small businesses were located within a block of this busy intersection. These included eight restaurants, seven dentists, four taverns, two drugstores, a theater, a used-car lot, a bakery, a jewelry store, a dry cleaner, and a shoe-repair shop.

Twin City Rapid Transit Company's Snelling Shops manufactured streetcars for the company's own use. The Snelling Shops also built streetcars for use in other American cities, including Duluth, Chicago, and Seattle. After TCRT eliminated streetcars in 1954, the shops were demolished. Allianz Field now occupies this site. (Courtesy of the Minnesota Streetcar Museum.)

Ray-Bell Films traces its origins to 1914, when an early St. Paul movie operator, Charles Bell, teamed up with two St. Paul partners to make promotional films for the Northern Pacific Railroad. In 1915, Bell's company relocated to this University Avenue building. The business was renamed Ray-Bell when Reid Ray, a film technician, joined the firm.

Over its 50-year history, Ray-Bell filmed at locations all over the country and used its University Avenue facility for in-studio filming and processing. A camera crew is shown preparing a film shoot for a clothing advertisement. In the mid-1940s, Ray-Bell outgrew its University Avenue location and relocated to a new facility on Ford Parkway. The company closed in the early 1970s.

This University Avenue building served as the headquarters for the Brown and Bigelow Company. The St. Paul firm, founded in 1896, produced calendars, playing cards, and other promotional materials. Prominent illustrators—including Norman Rockwell—designed artwork for the company's products. A section of the University Avenue building has been preserved and repurposed for use as offices. Today, Brown and Bigelow continues to produce company-branded promotional materials at a plant on St. Paul's West Side.

FOOD FIGHTS FOR FREEDOM

We proudly hail the greatest army in the world-- 30 million American farmers -- producing the FOOD that is winning today's battles -- FOOD that will write tomorrow's peace in a hungering world.

FIGHTERS ON THE FARMS...
WE SALUTE YOU!

BROWN & BIGELOW
Remembrance Advertising
ST. PAUL 4, MINN.

During World War II, Brown and Bigelow Company incorporated patriotic themes into its products. This poster, entitled "Food Fights for Freedom," declares: "We proudly hail the greatest army in the world, the 30 million American farmers producing the food that is winning today's battles."

Owens Motor Sales was one of St. Paul's early Ford dealerships. University Avenue was just beginning to emerge as St. Paul's auto row when this photograph was taken in 1918. The Owens building is still in use today. Remodeling has added a second story, but the distinctive arched windows in the original building have been retained.

Model T Fords were the cars of choice for motorists driving up and down University Avenue in this 1932 photograph. This intersection with Rice Street was later cleared to make room for the expansion of the commercial district adjacent to the Minnesota State Capitol.

St. Paul business owners were able to network at the North Central Commercial Club in 1929. The club attracted a contingent of politicians from the capitol, which was located just a few blocks away. The building next to the North Central Commercial Club is the Ford Motor Company's St. Paul assembly plant.

In 1914, Ford established this assembly plant and service center for its Model T cars. That same year, the company built a large manufacturing plant across the river in Minneapolis. Both facilities were replaced by the Twin Cities Assembly Plant in St. Paul's Highland Park district in 1925. In recent years, the University Avenue plant has been used as an office building for state agencies.

Five

COMMUNITY CORRIDOR

When University Avenue began to develop as a major commercial corridor in the 1890s, the street attracted numerous small businesses serving people living in the adjacent neighborhoods. Up and down the street, residents could find block after block of grocery stores, cafés, barbershops, haberdasheries, and other businesses catering to their day-to-day needs. During the early decades of the 20th century, with the emergence of the automotive and motion picture industries, University Avenue became the place to go to buy a car or see a movie.

By 1916, University Avenue was the home of a group of early theaters, including the Victoria, Como, Hamline, and Faust. The street's role as St. Paul's auto row began early in the 20th century, when the first automobile dealers began to appear on University Avenue. Over the next two decades, more than 20 dealerships would locate along the avenue.

Many neighborhood businesses were clustered in the commercial nodes formed at the intersections where the north–south arterial streets connected with University Avenue. In Minneapolis, these included Central Avenue NE and Fourteenth Avenue SE. In St. Paul, major commercial nodes were created at Raymond, Snelling, Lexington, Dale, and Rice Streets.

Through the 1950s, University Avenue continued to serve as the major destination for Twin Citians who came to the intercity thoroughfare to work, shop, and play. The street's fortunes began in decline in the 1960s, when a new intercity freeway, Interstate 94, connected the downtown areas of the Twin Cities. The decline was offset, at least in part, when new arrivals to Minnesota—many of whom came from Southeast Asia—injected fresh entrepreneurial energy into the corridor's St. Paul section.

Minneapolis's Jax Café traces its origins to 1920, when Stanley Kozlak opened a dance hall in a two-story commercial building at the corner of University Avenue and Twentieth Street. After the end of Prohibition in 1933, the Kozlak family converted the building to a bar and restaurant that soon became a popular northeast Minneapolis destination. The Kozlak family continues to own and operate this iconic University Avenue eatery. (Courtesy of Hennepin County Library Special Collections.)

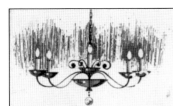

Welcome to Jax cafe
the Kozlaks

THE ULTIMATE IN PRIVATE PARTY FACILITIES

Five beautifully appointed dining rooms from which to choose. Jax offers the ultimate in private party facilities for groups of 15 - 400 guests. Dinner meeting, reception, reunion; luncheon or dinner. When you think of a party, think of Jax. The success of your function is our primary concern.

COSMOPOLITAN ROOM
(100 - 400 guests): Paneled in rich Cherrywood with massive beamed ceilings. Heavily carpeted except for Maplewood dance area. Serviced by two bars. Contains stage, public address system and all necessary audio visual props you may find necessary. Room offers impressive view of Jax Old World Garden.

JAX ROUND TABLE ROOM
(25-120 guests): Ideal for business groups that require absolute privacy and solid wall soundproofing. Swedish fireplace, private bar, oak paneled walls, and heavily carpeted.

JAX GARDEN ROOM
(15 - 40 guests): Overlooking the Old World Garden. Ideal for groups such as grooms dinners, family reunion and small conferences.

JAX CELTIC ROOM
(25 - 72 guests): Completely private and acoustically treated. Private bar. Fully carpeted. Rich butternut wall treatment.

Our Parents

In 1943 our parents purchased a business at the address called Jax. The seating was 6 and it was located in the area that now main bar. Mother and Dad set high standards for all employees set to work. Years Dad was purchasing agent, personnel director, managing manager, occasionally cook and sometimes caterer. Mother helped in the kitchen and even developed some of the salad dressings that are in use today. Their efforts met with great acceptance by the public and in ten years time Jax Cafe covered the entire main floor of the present building.

Today Jax is a two-story restaurant famed for its cuisine.

Jax has been visited and revisited by guests from practically every nation on earth. The reputation of the restaurant has been built and maintained on

1. The finest U. S. choice and prime beef, aged to perfection and prepared to your specification.
2. Selected seafoods from the great ports of the world as well as superb fresh water fish from Minnesota, Canada, and our garden stream.
3. Unusual and exotic foods of the world featured on Jax specialty nights and at luncheon.

We are fortunate to have our father and our mother on hand to help us maintain these standards.

JACK and BILL KOZLAK

Jax Kitchens

Jax has not one but two of America's most modern restaurant kitchens. Sparkling pastel tile reaches from floor to ceiling and gleaming stainless steel equipment is at the command of Jax chefs. The electronic stainless steel dishwashers automatically wash and rinse every piece of china and silver at 180 degrees. Jax can serve speedily and efficiently as many as 400 guests from the second floor kitchen without interfering in any way with the tempo of service on the ground floor. This is one big reason why Jax can say "The ultimate in private party facilities."

With its steaks, prime ribs, and shrimp cocktails, Jax Café provided classic supper-club fare in the 1950s. This menu from that era lists an hors d'oeuvres tray for two for $3.00 and a T-bone steak with a tossed salad and a baked potato for $5.50. (Courtesy of Hennepin County Library Special Collections.)

These houses on University Avenue are typical of the modest frame dwellings built near the start of the 20th century in northeast Minneapolis neighborhoods. Homes liked these housed the thousands of Eastern and Southern European immigrants who flocked to the Twin Cities to work in the city's mills and factories. In recent years, a new generation of neighborhood residents, many of whom work in the arts, are rehabing these still-sturdy homes that are now more than 120 years old. (Both, courtesy of Hennepin County Library Special Collections.)

Emily's has been a favorite Twin Cities destination for Middle Eastern cuisine since 1973. The no-frills deli and restaurant operates out of a modest storefront building at Sixth Street and University Avenue. House specialties include cabbage rolls, stuffed grape leaves, and lamb shish kebab. (Courtesy of the author.)

Reflecting the northeast Minneapolis area's history as a home for Eastern European immigrants, a number of churches with European ties are located along a six-block stretch of Northeast University Avenue. St. Constantine Ukrainian Catholic Church is part of that group. The congregation formed in 1913 to serve the area's growing population of Ukrainian immigrants. The current St. Constantine's, with its distinctive Byzantine dome, was built in 1972. (Both, courtesy of Hennepin County Library Special Collections.)

St. Anthony High-Rise, built in 1963, provides housing for low-income seniors and people with disabilities. The building is part of a system of nearly 6,000 housing units operated by the Minneapolis Public Housing Authority. Public housing residents, including those in this building, generally pay 30 percent of their monthly income for rent. (Courtesy of Hennepin County Library Special Collections.)

This northeast Minneapolis landmark was established by Wasyl Kramarczuk and his wife, Anna, who emigrated to the United States from their native Ukraine in 1948. Wasyl brought with him sausage-making skills that he had acquired in his Eastern European homeland. Over its 75-year history, Kramarczuk Deli's handmade sausages and fresh-baked bread and pastries have created a large and loyal customer base. (Courtesy of the author.)

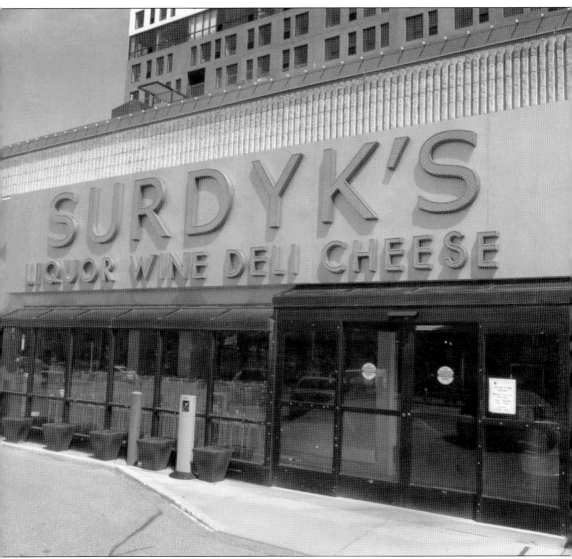

Surdyk's has deep roots in northeast Minneapolis. The family patriarch, Joseph Surdyk, established the business in 1934, soon after the end of Prohibition. His first liquor store was located down the block from Surdyk's current University Avenue location. Joseph's grandson, Jim Surdyk, now owns and operates the family business. (Courtesy of the author.)

Considered the oldest existing building in Minneapolis, the Ard Godfrey House, which dates to 1849, was originally located on Main Street. The house was later moved to its current site on University Avenue. The Ard Godfrey House is operated as a museum and historic site by the Women's Club of Minneapolis. (Courtesy of Hennepin County Library Special Collections.)

Here, a modern office tower looms over the Ard Godfrey House. In the foreground, a docent is dressed in a 19th-century costume. (Courtesy of Hennepin County Library Special Collections.)

Built near the beginning of the 20th century, the Beaux Arts–style Pillsbury Library was named for Minneapolis industrialist and community leader John S. Pillsbury. Located at the corner of University and Central Avenues, the library was in use between 1904 and 1967. In more recent times, the historic building has been used as an art gallery and an office building. (Courtesy of Hennepin County Library Special Collections.)

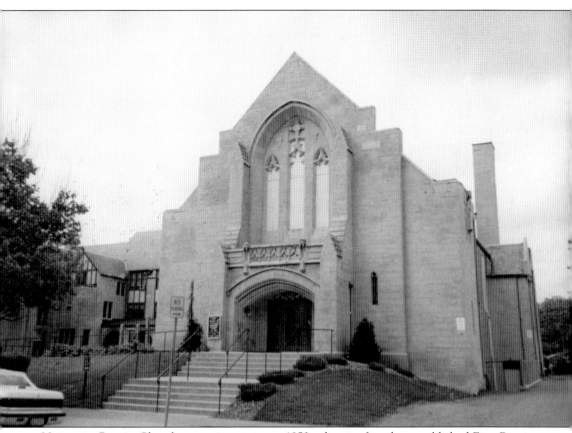

University Baptist Church traces its origins to 1850, when its founders established First Baptist Church in what was then the village of St. Anthony. The current church building was constructed in 1921. It includes a 250-seat sanctuary, a Dobson pipe organ, a gymnasium, and a wing with offices and meeting rooms. (Courtesy of Hennepin County Library Special Collections.)

Florence Court is one of University Avenue's oldest residential developments still in use today. Constructed as a series of interconnected brick buildings, Florence Court was built in 1886, with improvements added in 1921 and 1929. Over the years, Florence Court was subdivided into 40 apartments, providing cheap housing for generations of University of Minnesota students. The complex has been substantially upgraded in recent years. (Courtesy of Hennepin County Library Special Collections.)

Bounded by University Avenue at Fourteenth Avenue SE, Dinkytown's shops and restaurants have been serving the community since the dawn of the 20th century. The origins of the district's name are shrouded in mystery. One theory says Dinkytown is a reference to a small locomotive called a dinkey that ran on the nearby railroad tracks. (Courtesy of Hennepin County Library Special Collections.)

In recent years, Dinkytown's historic ambience has been under threat as massive new apartment buildings continue to encroach on the district. A longtime neighborhood icon, Annie's Parlor, closed in 2020. (Courtesy of Hennepin County Library Special Collections.)

A fixture at Fourteenth and University Avenue for 75 years, Perines Bookstore served as the gateway to Dinkytown. Perines sold new and used textbooks to generations of University of Minnesota students. Along with textbooks, the store specialized in imported foreign language publications. Perines closed in the 1970s. More recently, a popular campus restaurant, Annie's Parlor, occupied the former Perines space. Annie's closed in 2020. (Courtesy of Hennepin County Library Special Collections.)

The Tea House is the "best Chinese restaurant in the Twin Cities," according to Jon Cheng, a food critic for the *Star Tribune*. The restaurant "embraces the south of China's regional cuisine and nails it," Cheng says. Located on University Avenue near the east end of the Minneapolis campus, the Tea House is a popular gathering spot for University of Minnesota students and faculty. (Courtesy of the author.)

Called the Witch's Hat by community residents, this 106-foot water tower was built in 1906 to improve water access for the adjacent Prospect Park neighborhood. By the 1950s, the imposing structure had become functionally obsolete. When the Minneapolis Water Department announced plans to demolish the tower, neighborhood residents rallied to support it and succeeded in preserving the much-loved community landmark. (Courtesy of Hennepin County Library Special Collections.)

Prospect Park traces its history to the 1890s, when it was developed as an "intown suburb" served by the Interurban streetcar line. A popular residential location for University of Minnesota faculty, Prospect Park contains well-preserved housing stock and offers a bucolic setting that continues to attract newcomers. The neighborhood's strategic location at the center of the Twin Cities metro area and its direct access to light rail transit adds to its popularity. (Courtesy of Hennepin County Library Special Collections.)

These two trolley cars made their final University Avenue run in 1954 as TCRT began dismantling the region's streetcar system. That year, on July 24, the company took local VIPs on a ceremonial final ride through downtown Minneapolis to the Snelling Shops in St. Paul. There, company head Fred Ossanna delivered a coup de grace by lighting one of the cars on fire. (Courtesy of the Minnesota Streetcar Museum.)

After TCRT eliminated streetcars in 1954, workers began removing tracks from University Avenue. Later, the tracks were at the center of a major corruption scandal when TCRT head Fred Ossanna was tried and convicted of receiving kickbacks from a local scrap dealer.

Iris Park, now a small patch of greenery on University Avenue, dates to the 1880s. The pond in this 1924 photograph remains the park's focal point today. Iris Park was once part of a much larger recreation area that included a dance pavilion, bandstand, and merry-go-round.

Midway Hospital utilized a unique Y-shaped design when the hospital was built in 1926. The design enabled hospital staff to manage patient care from a central location on each floor. Midway continued to provide hospital services from its University Avenue location until 1997, when the facility was closed and converted to a medical office building.

Gordon Parks High School serves at-risk St. Paul students who may be struggling academically at a more standard secondary school. When the educational program opened in 1991, it occupied rental space in the Unidale Mall. The school soon outgrew that location, prompting the St. Paul Board of Education to approve the construction of this new building in 2007. Like many of the school's current students, Gordon Parks struggled with academics during his formative years in St. Paul. (Courtesy of the author.)

Renowned photographer, author, and director Gordon Parks grew up in St. Paul. He got his start in fashion photography at Frank Murphy's, an upscale women's clothing store in downtown St. Paul. Parks was honored by the City of St. Paul when it named this University Avenue high school after him.

Spruce Tree Centre occupies the southwest corner of Snelling and University Avenues, St. Paul's most heavily travelled intersection. Spruce Tree Centre's green-tiled facade has given it a prominent presence on University Avenue. In recent years, Spruce Tree's strategic location at the Snelling Avenue LRT station has boosted occupancy rates. The site deserves a historic footnote—in 1932, a gangland murder occurred there, according to St. Paul historian Paul Macabee. (Courtesy of the author.)

A neighborhood icon for more than 50 years, Midway Used and Rare Books helps anchor the busy intersection at Snelling and University Avenues. The store specializes in science fiction, photography, art, and philosophy, along with a large collection of new and used comic books. The family-owned business started as a small paperback exchange in the 1960s. Today, it has become one of the largest booksellers in the Midwest, with an inventory of more than 50,000 volumes. (Courtesy of Ramsey County Historical Society.)

For nearly 90 years, Midway Chevrolet was a fixture on St. Paul's auto row. That history came to an end in 2007, when Midway relocated to a new site in Maplewood. Like its competitors, Midway was unable to withstand the draw of suburbia. A suburban location gave the dealer closer proximity to its customers and the opportunity to build a larger and more modern sales and servicing facility.

These new arrivals to Minnesota are studying to become US citizens at the Hmong Cultural Center on University Avenue. Several dozen Hmong organizations and businesses are now located along the avenue's east end. Today, St. Paul has one of the country's largest populations of Hmong Americans. (Courtesy of Hmong Cultural Center.)

In 1955, this sign on University Avenue at Snelling Avenue identified the future site of Midway Center, one of St. Paul's earliest strip commercial centers. The sign declared that Midway would be "a complete one stop retail center with everything you need or want." The center, anchored by a Rainbow Grocery Store, was intended to help University Avenue contend with the economic fallout caused by the construction of Interstate 94. Midway Center was badly damaged during the civil unrest that followed the murder of George Floyd by a Minneapolis Police Department officer in 2020. In 2021, the center was demolished.

The Faust, at University Avenue and Dale Street, had a 60-year history as a first-run movie theater. But the suburban boom took a toll on the inner-city theater. By the 1970s, the Faust had become an X-rated theater. The man shown here with his young daughter was part of a group of neighborhood activists who picketed the shabby porn palace in the 1980s. Eventually, the Faust was demolished and replaced by the Rondo Community Library. (Courtesy of the *Star Tribune*.)

One of the few Black-owned businesses on University Avenue in the 1950s and 1960s, Road Buddy's was a restaurant and nightclub at the corner of University Avenue and Avon Street. The restaurant's owner, Clyde Odum, operated a music venue known as the Ebony Lounge on the building's second floor. For a time in the 1960s, radio station KUXL broadcast an R&B musical program from the Ebony Lounge. The former Road Buddy's space is now occupied by the Ngon Bistro restaurant.

One of St. Paul's oldest congregations still active today, Christ Lutheran Church on Capitol Hill traces its origins to 1868. Originally known as the Norwegian Evangelical Lutheran Church when it was built in 1913, it was later renamed in reference to its location across from the Minnesota State Capitol.

This medical facility was known as St. Paul Ramsey County Hospital when this photograph was taken in 1970. Then a 100-year-old public agency, the hospital had recently moved to a new campus on University Avenue. In 1994, the hospital was acquired by the nonprofit Health Partners. Today, the medical center is known as Regions Hospital.

Six

A New Century

University Avenue has been caught up in a building boom during the early decades of the 21st century. The boom has been propelled, in large part, by the new light rail transit (LRT) line that connects the Minneapolis and St. Paul central business districts. Initially known as the Central Corridor and then renamed the Green Line, the LRT mainly follows the same University Avenue route used by the Interurban streetcar line more than a century ago.

Construction began in 2011 on the $957-million project and took three years to be completed. The construction period caused serious hardships for scores of small businesses along University Avenue, many of which were owned by immigrants. These businesses lost sales and customers when the roadway and sidewalks in front of their shops were torn up for months at a time. Nonprofit business development organizations were able to offset this economic fallout by offering forgivable loans to businesses located on University Avenue.

During the planning phase, the LRT generated opposition from community activists along the corridor who maintained that the proposed project did not adequately serve their neighborhoods. As a result of these protests, the Metropolitan Council, which operates the system, agreed to add three new LRT stations to the original plan. According to information provided by the council, the Green Line has generated over $3 billion in investments, with more than 20,000 apartment units completed or under development.

A decorative mural enlivens the front of Las Estrellas School at the corner of University Avenue and West Broadway in Minneapolis. Originally known as Sheridan Elementary School, this neighborhood landmark was renamed Las Estrellas to better reflect the school's diversity. The name means "the stars" in Spanish. (Courtesy of the author.)

The 1928 Ritz Theater anchors a key arts hub at Thirteenth Street and University Avenue that is part of the broader Northeast Minneapolis Arts District. In 1936, the building's Art Deco makeover made it a much-admired community landmark. Today, the Ritz is the home of Theater Latte Da.

This glass-encased mixed-use development replaced the Eastgate Shopping Center, which was demolished in 2004. Known as the Cobalt for the blue cast of its facade, the development contains 93 condominiums. A Lunds & Byerlys grocery store occupies the building's first floor. (Both, courtesy of the author.)

New high-rise apartments in and around East Hennepin and University Avenues are transforming this historic commercial district. Over the last five years, more than 1,000 apartment units have been added to the district's housing stock. Even with the real estate boom, landmark businesses such as Surdyk's and Kramarczuk Deli's are helping to maintain the neighborhood's historic feel.

The McNamara Alumni Center was designed by Antoine Pedock, a New Mexico architect who specializes in naturalistic structures that appear to rise up from the ground. Architectural historian Larry Millett says that the building resembles "a giant, granite sheathed geode." Millett notes that its "predominant quality seems to be a kind of rockbound chill." (Courtesy of the author.)

Huntington Bank Stadium is now the home of the University of Minnesota's Golden Gophers football team. Construction of the 50,000-seat stadium began in 2006 and was completed in 2009. The Minnesota Tribal Nations Plaza, which flanks the stadium's western entrance, honors Minnesota's 11 tribal nations. (Courtesy of the author.)

Detroit-based First Independence Bank now occupies the University Avenue building that originally housed a Wells Fargo branch. First Independence Bank is the first Black-owned financial institution to do business in Minnesota. (Courtesy of Terry Faust.)

Damon Jenkins, the senior vice president of First Independence Bank, says he hopes the company will be a "beacon of hope" for the Twin Cities' Black community. "It is an opportunity for our community to have its own institution, something that can be a source of pride for our people." (Courtesy of Terry Faust.)

The Dubliner, a University Avenue fixture since 1983, has brought a touch of Ireland to St. Paul's Midway District. This neighborhood pub is known for its wide selection of draft beer and top-shelf whiskey. The Dubliner features Irish and American music six nights a week and Irish dance lessons on Wednesday nights. (Courtesy of the author.)

Initially known as the Central Corridor and then renamed the Green Line, this light rail transit project follows the same University Avenue route used by the Interurban streetcar line more than 100 years ago. This 2010 photograph shows a section of the rail line under construction at University Avenue and Highway 280.

According to its website, Twin Cities Habitat for Humanity works to bring affordable housing to Twin Cities communities and the families that live in them. The organization "builds, repairs, and sells homes to families with an affordable mortgage while connecting them to the community through neighborhood revitalization projects." (Both, courtesy of Twin Cities Habitat for Humanity.)

One of St. Paul's most unusual public spaces, Dickerman Park fronts a three-block stretch of University Avenue between Fairview and Aldine Streets. Only about 100 feet wide, the park appears to function as the front yard for a series of private office buildings set back from the street. In 2015, the City of St. Paul overhauled Dickerman Park by constructing walkways and installing new landscaping. (Courtesy of the author.)

Located at the Fairview LRT station, Episcopal Church Home (ECH) provides a continuum of residential care for older adults. In 1920, ECH built its first permanent facility on its current University Avenue campus. ECH's most recent expansion occurred in 2012 with the construction of a 170-unit addition on the former Porky's Drive-In site. (Both, courtesy of Episcopal Church Home.)

During the civil unrest following the murder of George Floyd in 2020, more than 100 businesses along University Avenue in St. Paul were either destroyed or badly damaged. In these photographs, an area resident surveys the damage (above) while a work crew boards up the windows on a vandalized building (below). The Midway Chamber of Commerce and other local community groups are heading recovery efforts along University Avenue. (Both, courtesy of *Midway Como Frogtown Monitor.*)

Allianz Field is a soccer stadium built for the Minnesota United FC soccer club, known as the Loons. The stadium opened in 2019 on the site of the former St. Paul bus barn. Allianz Field's unique architecture consists of a ring-shaped structure that seats about 19,000 fans. A glasslike mesh material wraps around the stadium, giving it an undulating feel. (Courtesy of the author.)

This now-vacant building was occupied by a Montgomery Ward store when the building was constructed in 1995 as part of the Midway Marketplace development, which now occupies the original Wards site. The building included a 70-foot tower intended to evoke the original 257-foot tower built in 1921 as part of Wards' large retail and distribution center. The 1995 Wards store was replaced by a Herberger's that is now closed. (Courtesy of the author.)

Wilder Foundation's corporate headquarters occupies the former Lexington Park site on University Avenue. The foundation is named for Amherst H. Wilder, whose bequest launched the charitable organization in 1906. The foundation has maintained the Wilder family's commitment to serving St. Paul's poor, elderly, and ailing populations. (Courtesy of the author.)

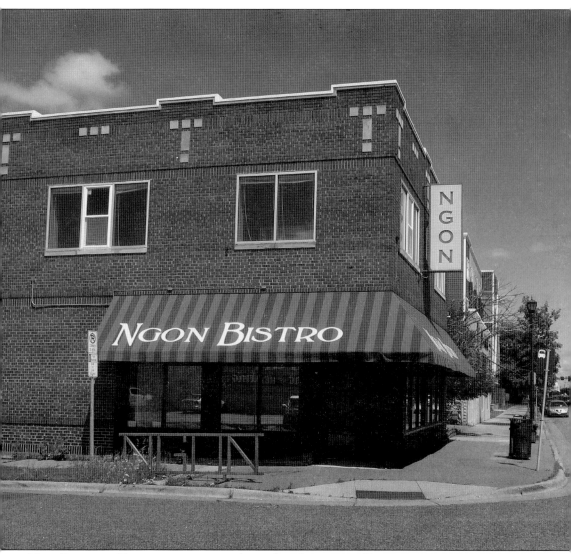

Ngon Bistro is a Vietnamese restaurant located at the corner of University Avenue and Avon Street in the Frogtown neighborhood. The restaurant adds a French touch to its traditional Southeast Asian cuisine. Ngon Bistro's signature pho, the traditional Vietnamese soup, comes with beef, chicken, or meatballs. (Courtesy of the author.)

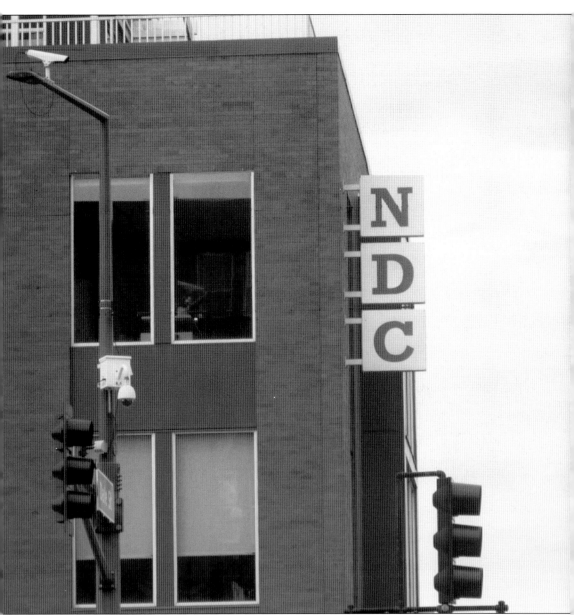

Neighborhood Development Center (NDC) was established in 1993 and provides technical support and financing for small businesses in the Twin Cities. In the early 2000s, NDC spearheaded efforts to assist businesses impacted by the light rail transit construction on University Avenue. Since 1993, the nonprofit organization has provided $26 million in financing to nearly 1,000 borrowers. (Courtesy of the author.)

The metal panels displayed on the Dale Street LRT station represent the different cultural groups that have settled in the surrounding neighborhoods. The art installation, entitled *Crossroads Again*, was created by Sietu Jones. This panel highlights African culture. (Courtesy of the author.)

The Rondo Community Outreach Library was built in 2006 on the site of the former Faust theater at Dale Street and University Avenue. The library commemorates Rondo, the largely African American neighborhood that was destroyed during the construction of Interstate 94. The upper floors of the library building provide 98 units of affordable housing. (Courtesy of the author.)

This mixed-use development at the northeast corner of Dale Street and University Avenue is known as Frogtown Square. The project includes Los Ocampo restaurant and several other community-based businesses. Frogtown Square was developed by the nonprofit Neighborhood Development Center. The upper floors consist of 48 units of affordable housing operated by Episcopal Homes. (Courtesy of the author.)

This 68-unit affordable housing project, known as Western U Plaza, incorporates the 1912 building constructed for the Old Home Dairy. The building had been vacant for 10 years before it was purchased and repurposed by two local housing organizations, Aurora St. Anthony Neighborhood Development Corporation and the Sand Companies. Western U Plaza is located across from the Western Avenue station on the Green Line LRT. (Courtesy of the author.)

This stainless-steel dragon-like shape embellishes the Green Line LRT station at Western Avenue. The art celebrates St. Paul's large Southeast Asian community, which has done much to rejuvenate this stretch of University Avenue. The installation, known as *River Dragon*, was created by Catherine Widgery. (Courtesy of the author.)

This multitenant development helps identify University Avenue's east end as a center of Hmong entrepreneurialism. The Hmong Minnesota Professionals building houses a chiropractic clinic, a dental practice, an insurance agency, and an attorney's office. These businesses demonstrate the progress made by the Hmong community since its members first arrived in Minnesota as refugees in the 1970s. (Courtesy of the author.)

Over a four-year period from 2013 to 2017, the Minnesota State Capitol was closed while the 130-year-old building was overhauled and renovated. Three craftsmen are shown preparing to add a final layer of gold leaf on the finial, the decorative structure that sits on top of the capitol dome. (Courtesy of Tom Olmscheid.)

The *Quadringa* sculpture serves as the backdrop for this photograph of construction workers renovating the capitol dome. The *Quadringa* depicts four horses puling a chariot driven by a heroic figure. The sculpture is intended to represent the progress of the state of Minnesota. Noted American sculptor Daniel Chester French created the dramatic work. (Courtesy of Tom Olmscheid.)

BIBLIOGRAPHY

Diers, John W., and Aaron Isaacs. *Twin Cities by Trolley: The Streetcar Era in Minneapolis and St. Paul*. Minneapolis: University of Minnesota Press, 2007.

Gardner, Dennis. *Our Minnesota State Capitol*. St. Paul: Minnesota Historical Society Press, 2017.

Kieley, Genny Zak, and Nancy Doerfler. "Northeast Minneapolis: A Church on Every Corner." *Hennepin History* 57, No. 4 (1998): 4–21.

McClure, Jane. "Frogtown: An Introduction." Produced and directed by East End Productions, edited by Tony Andrea. *Saint Paul Historical*. Saintpaulhistorical.com/items/show/154.

———. "The Midway and Its Colorful History." *Ramsey County History*, Fall 1994.

McMahon, Brian. *The Ford Century in Minnesota*. Minneapolis: University of Minnesota Press, 2013.

Millett, Larry. *AIA Guide to the Twin Cities*. St. Paul: Minnesota Historical Society Press, 2007.

Rubenstein, Aaron. "Summary of Historical Significance of Nine Focus Buildings." St. Paul, MN: Historic St. Paul, 2013.

Thornley, Stew. *Historic Ballparks of the Twin Cities*. Charleston, SC: The History Press, 2021.

Twin Cities Public Television. "University Avenue: One Street, 1,000 Dreams." www.tpt.org/university-ave-one-street-1000-dreams/.

DISCOVER THOUSANDS OF LOCAL HISTORY BOOKS FEATURING MILLIONS OF VINTAGE IMAGES

Arcadia Publishing, the leading local history publisher in the United States, is committed to making history accessible and meaningful through publishing books that celebrate and preserve the heritage of America's people and places.

Find more books like this at
www.arcadiapublishing.com

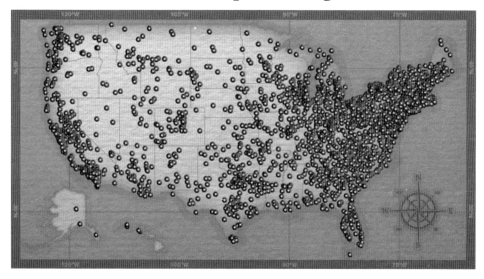

Search for your hometown history, your old stomping grounds, and even your favorite sports team.

Consistent with our mission to preserve history on a local level, this book was printed in South Carolina on American-made paper and manufactured entirely in the United States. Products carrying the accredited Forest Stewardship Council (FSC) label are printed on 100 percent FSC-certified paper.

MADE IN THE USA